THE STORY
OF
YOUR COAT

BY CLARA HOLLOS

Pictures by Herbert Kruckman

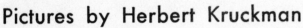

A Young World Book

This is the story of your coat.

Do you think your coat is just an ordinary coat? Wait until you hear its story.

Your coat is made of wool. The wool comes from sheep.

Let's see what happens to it before it becomes a coat.

You and I must take a long trip to find out. And we start at the other side of the world.

THE SHEEP RANCH

Here we are in Australia. Just look at this huge meadow covered with grass. And sheep, sheep everywhere. We are on a sheep ranch belonging to Mr. Tick.

Thousands of sheep graze under the bright sun. The best sheep with the finest wool come from Australia. Just touch their backs. How rich and soft their coats feel!

It's all wool.

THE BATH

The sheep are getting a bath. This is something special, for they are washed only twice a year. The sheep act as if they were taking a bath just for fun. Not at all, sheep! You are getting a shampoo before a haircut, just as people do in a barber shop.

When the sheep have been washed, the shepherd sees that they keep clean until the big day arrives.

THE SALE

The big day is here!   This is the day when the wool is sold.

The gentleman over here is Mr. Tack.   He is a buyer who has come all the way from the United States to buy wool from Mr. Tick in Australia.

The sheep are lined up, and Mr. Tack takes his choice.   Of course, he picks only the ones with the thickest, fluffiest coats. They give the best wool.

THE SHEARING

This place looks like a barber shop. But here the barber is called the shearer, and his scissors are called shears. The sheep shearer uses automatic shears which work like an electric razor.

Do you think it's easy to shear sheep? Not at all. Shorty, the shearer, has been working on this ranch ever since he was a little boy. No wonder he can do such a good job of shearing off a sheep's coat all in one piece.

After it is sheared, the sheep's coat is called the fleece. Each fleece is rolled into a bundle.

See how funny the sheep are without their woolly coats. They look all naked.

Well, we are sorry to leave the sheep, but we have other things to do.

SORTING AND SHIPPING

These men are sorting the bundles of fleece in a place called a sorting station. They separate the fleece into three piles—the "very-best," the "next-best," and the "not-so-good."

The packer puts fifty small bundles of fleece into a large bag. Each bag is put onto the scales to see how much it weighs. Then it gets a number—Number 1 for the "very-best," Number 2 for the "next-best," Number 3 for the "not-so-good."

Now all the bags are ready for shipping. They are loaded onto big trucks which line up in front of the sorting station.

Mr. Tack, the buyer, has finished his business in Australia. Before he goes, he pays Mr. Tick, the rancher, for the fleece.

Everybody says good-by to Mr. Tack. He can even hear the sheep baa-ing far away. By-byeeeee!

The trucks are ready to go to the harbor.

THE HARBOR

What an exciting place this is! We are in Sidney, the largest harbor in Australia. Big ships are coming in from far-off countries. Other big ships are sailing out of the harbor to all parts of the world.

Just look at that crowd of people—Australians, Chinese, Americans, and many others. Everybody is busy. Workers are unloading boxes, barrels, and bags from large trucks. These workers are called longshoremen. Many hands are busy with our bags of fleece. The place is buzzing. Rush, rush, rush!

Everybody is rushing except Mr. Tack. He is taking it easy now, because the shipping company will look after everything.

The boxes and barrels and bags that are loaded onto the ship are called the cargo.

Good-by, Australia, land of sheep and sunshine and wide meadows. We are sailing home to the United States.

It's good to be back on land after four weeks on the Pacific Ocean. This is the harbor of San Francisco, California. It's raining cats and dogs, but Mr. Tack is not worried, because the fleece is packed in waterproof bags.

Now the cargo is unloaded. Our bags of fleece are put on trucks to be taken to the railroad station.

The boxes and barrels and bags that are put on the train are called freight.

Mr. Tack is a busy businessman, so he takes an airplane.

THE WAREHOUSE

We arrive in Lawrence, Massachusetts, near Boston. This big building is a warehouse. Its walls are made of steel and other fireproof materials, for millions of dollars worth of goods are stored here. Some storage rooms are as large as a railroad station. Here the boxes and barrels and bags are kept until their owners need them.

Mr. Toe is the owner of the bags of fleece. He is a textile manufacturer, and he owns a factory where woolen cloth is made. Now Mr. Toe pays Mr. Tack for buying the wool.

Good-by, Mr. Tack. We won't see you again.

THE TEXTILE MILL

This is Mr. Toe's factory. It is a big place that takes up a whole block of buildings. It is called a textile mill, and the workers who run the machines here are called textile workers.

The bags of fleece have arrived from the warehouse, and the workers are ready to start. They have to work very hard to make nice woolen cloth out of that coarse, greasy fleece.

CLEANING AND COMBING

Here are some workers in the texile mill sorting the wool—Number 1, the "very-best"; Number 2, the "next-best"; Number 3, the "not-so-good." Mr. Toe is required by our government to keep the different kinds separate. If cloth is made from Number 3, the "not-so-good," he has to sell it cheaper than cloth made from Number 1, the "very-best," or Number 2, the "next-best." The "very-best" has to have a label that says "100 per cent pure wool."

Now comes the cleaning. The workers put the fleece in a machine where it is washed just like dirty laundry. They scour it with soap and chemicals until it is white and fluffy. It is dried by an electric fan.

Then a big machine with wire teeth combs the fleece. It takes the tangles out and makes the fleece smooth just as you smooth your hair with a comb.

But let's go on and see some very interesting work.

SPINNING

Yarn is wool thread out of which woolen cloth is made.

How is yarn made?

Take a piece of wool from your mother's knitting bag. Pick it apart until it is soft and fluffy. Now hold it in one hand. Keep twisting it round and round in the same direction with your other hand.

See, it's getting to look more and more like thread! The longer you twist it, the stronger the yarn will be.

The spinning machine works the same way. The machine has a part like a hand that holds the wool. This is the bobbin. It is stuck on the end of a rod called the spindle. A motor makes the spindle, with the bobbin, spin around faster and faster, twisting the wool tighter and tighter.

But this wonderful machine cannot make yarn by itself. It needs a worker to run it. Here is Spike, the spinner, who runs the spinning machine. Spike knows a great deal about the machine. He is going to night school to study textile engineering. What a good engineer he will be, because he already knows so much about spinning!

After the yarn has been twisted round and round until it is strong enough, it is wound onto large rolls.

Now it is ready to be woven.

THE LOOM

A loom is a weaving machine that makes cloth. It has little machine fingers, called heddles, that pick up first one thread and then another. These threads are the warp.

Have you ever watched the way your mother's needle goes in and out when she darns stockings? That's the way the shuttle goes. In and out between the warp threads, across and back, it carries a thread called the weft.

Here William, the weaver, puts the yarn on the heddles, the little machine fingers, to make the warp. Then he gets the shuttle ready to carry the weft. This takes a long time, but William knows his job well. All set? William starts the loom going. But his work is not over. He goes on to do the same thing to the next loom—and the next—and the next. He has to look after several looms at once.

William's father was also a weaver, and William himself has worked in a textile mill for many years.

Shuttle
weft
heddles raised
warp
heddles lowered

A hundred years ago, little children used to work in textile mills from sunrise until after dark in the evening. They had no time to play, no time to go to school. And all they got for their long, hard work was a few cents. Their parents worked in the mills too. They were all very poor, very tired, and often hungry.

Finally, these grown-ups and children of long ago became so tired and hungry that they could stand it no longer. They decided to stick by each other to try and make life better for them all. They formed a group which they called a union and agreed not to work until all of them got more money. Of course, the looms could not run without workers. So at last the mill owners gave in.

After this fight, the workers did not have to work from sunrise until after dark. They had more time to talk with their children. They earned more money, too, so their children could leave the mills and go to school.

Ever since that time, their union has kept on making life better for the textile workers. William's father was a member of the union when he worked in the mill and today William is, too.

Now the first loom has finished weaving the yarn to cloth. Other workers, called examiners, go over every inch of cloth very carefully. They take out lumpy knots in the yarn and mend little holes. At last the cloth is perfect.

THE DYEING ROOM

The wool fabric is ready to be colored. We call this dyeing.

Many years ago, before machines were invented, only rich people could have beautifully colored cloth for their coats.

The colors, or dyes, were made out of vegetable roots, the bark of trees, berries, seeds, and even insects. Some colors were more expensive than others. A doctor, a lawyer, a merchant, a farmer all wore clothes of a different color. You could tell at once what a person did for a living just by looking at the color of his coat. Purple dye was made out of tiny shellfish. It was so hard and expensive to make that only the kings and princes had purple coats.

And oh, how mysterious the dye-makers were about the way they made their colors! Imagine a father on his death-bed saying to his son, "Dear son, I leave to you the big secret of how to make canary-yellow dye!"

Nowadays dyes are made in chemical laboratories by scientists. And you don't have to be a prince to have a purple coat!

Here is Clarence, the colorist, in his laboratory. He knows more about colors and dyes than any of those old-timers. And what he knows is no secret either. Clarence understands chemistry very well. He knows how to make purple dye not from rare shellfish but from ordinary coal tar.

Dick, the dyer, is a very important man, too. He puts the wool fabric in the dyeing vat, which is just like an enormous pot. He has to know exactly how many hours the fabric must boil in the vat of dye. Some dyes take a long time to color certain fabrics; others take only a short time. If Dick didn't know which —what a mess of spoiled cloth there would be!

Now we are in the drying and pressing room. First, the wet fabric is dried by hot air. Then Pete, the presser, draws the fabric between big, hot rollers until it is flat and smooth.

The finished fabric is measured by the yard. Then it is rolled into huge rolls called bolts. Each bolt gets a label with a number—Number 1 for the "very-best," Number 2 for the "next-best," and Number 3 for the "not-so-good."

It's time to say good-by to Spike and William, Clarence and Dick and Pete. We are now ready to take a trip to the biggest city in the world.

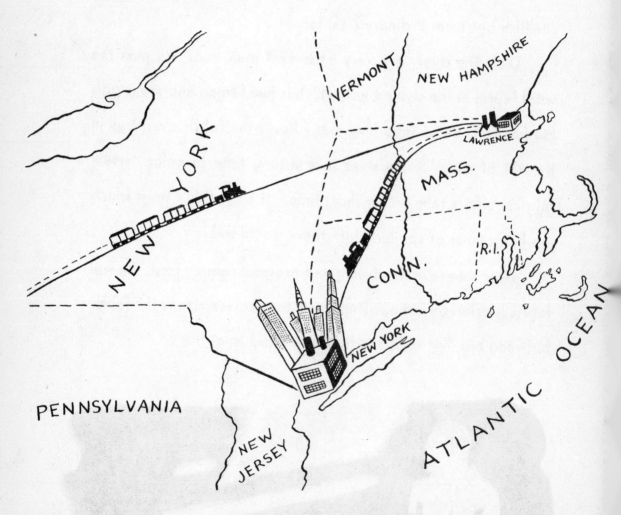

THE CLOTHING FACTORY

We are in New York City. In this building there is a factory where children's coats are made. It belongs to Mr. Bing who has just bought hundreds of bolts of woolen fabric from Mr. Toe's textile mill. The factory is in full swing, for many people want to buy children's coats. There are workers of many different nationalities—Jewish, Italian, Irish and others—all busy.

Let's go in and see what everybody is doing.

MAKING THE PATTERN

Up we go in a big elevator to the third floor. First we shall visit Doris, the designer. She knows all about children's coats— how they are put together and which styles look nicest. Doris studied designing in art school before she came to work for Mr. Bing.

Here is the new fabric. Doris likes it. It is Number 1, the "very-best." She looks at it for a long time. Flash! She has an idea. She draws a picture. What a handsome coat!

She calls in Pat, the pattern-maker. He makes a life-size drawing of the coat on pieces of paper which are as long as a person. He figures out how big size 8 has to be, and size 9, and size 10. Then he cuts out all the parts of the drawing and pins them together. Now he has a paper coat that looks just like Doris' picture. This is the pattern from which the cloth coats will be made.

Doris and Pat are pleased. They call in Mr. Bing, and he okays the design.

Mr. Bing wants to make money by selling these coats. That's his business. He figures out how much it will cost to make them—so much money for fabric, so much for buttons and thread. Now comes the question of how much he must pay the workers for making the coats.

And of course, the workers want to earn enough money to buy nice coats for their children like the ones they make. They want enough money to live in nice houses, eat good food, and go to the movies once in a while. They don't want to work so hard and fast that they are too tired to speak to their children in the evening.

Remember how the workers in the textile mill helped themselves by joining a union and working together to make life better for them all? The workers in Mr. Bing's factory belong to a union, too. They hold a meeting and choose Olga, one of the best workers in the sewing room, to speak for them all and tell Mr. Bing how many coats they can make in a day and how much money they think they should get for making them. Mr. Bing and Olga argue back and forth for a long time. At last they agree. The workers will make so many coats in one day, and each worker will get a certain amount of money for a day's work.

Now that's done, and we can follow Olga down to the workrooms on the second floor.

THE CUTTING ROOM

Our first stop is the cutting room where the fabric is cut into pieces.

The man who knows most about this job is Carl, the cutter. He is here, there, everywhere. He spreads the bolts of fabric on long tables. He puts the paper patterns on top of the fabric and outlines them with white chalk. The wool fabric is now ready to be cut—not with scissors, but with electric cutting machines,

that look like big knives. They can cut through many layers of
fabric all at once. You have to know your job when you handle
those big knives. See how carefully Carl does it. It looks easy,
but do you really think it is?

Every cutter cuts a different piece of the coat. Hyman
cuts the backs, Joe the fronts. Tony cuts the collars, Sammy
the pockets. Ivan cuts the right sleeves, and Jim the left ones.

Carl takes the pieces to the sewing room.

THE SEWING ROOM

When we say "sewing room," we mean a huge hall with rows and rows of electric sewing machines. The sewing-machine workers are called operators.

The worker who knows the most about this job is Olga, the operator. We met her before, remember? She can make the

pieces of cloth whizz under the needle of the sewing machine so fast that you think it must be magic.

Each operator sews a different part of the coat. Katie sews the backs and fronts together. Myrtle sews in the sleeves. Sarah sews on the collar, and Sonia the pockets. Betty sews up the hem, Mary puts in the lining. Stitch, stitch, stitch—the coat is done.

If one person had to make this coat by hand—s-t-i-t-c-h, s-t-i-t-c-h, s-t-i-t-c-h—it would take days.

If Olga had to make a whole coat by herself, it would still take from morning till night.

But when all the workers work together on electric sewing machines, a coat is done in a very short time.

FINISHING

Now the coats are ready for finishing. Fanny, the finisher, takes care of that. Zip, zip, the coats go under the buttonhole machine. Zing, zang, the buttons are put on—you guessed it, also by machine.

Now the coats are ready. A checker looks at each one to make sure nothing is wrong. Onto the racks they go. Hundreds of coats every day. Little coats and big coats. Girls' coats and boys' coats. Red coats and blue coats. And every coat has a label—Number 1 for the "very-best," Number 2 for the "next-best," and Number 3 for the "not-so-good."

Mr. Bing's order clerk is on the telephone. She has an order. Please send two hundred children's coats to Mr. Bang, who has a department store.

Yes, sir. Thank you. The order will be delivered on time.

Good-by, Carl. Good-by, Olga.

THE DEPARTMENT STORE

Here is the Bang department store.   A big sale is going on. What a crowd!   Everybody wants to buy children's coats.

Look out.   Don't push!   Here we are.   Which coat do you want?   The yellow one?   Fine, let's try it on.   It fits perfectly. How much does it cost?   We buy it.

It is marked Number 1, the "very best."

The coat is made of wool.

The wool came from sheep.

It came from Australia to the United States, from Sidney to San Francisco. From San Francisco to Lawrence. From Lawrence to New York.

It traveled by truck, by ship, by train.

It was cargo.   It was freight.

It was on a ranch.

It was in a warehouse.

It was in a textile mill.

It was in a clothing factory.

It was in a department store.

It was fleece.

It was yarn.

It was fabric.

It was sheared.

It was weighed.

It was packed.

It was cleaned.

It was spun.

It was woven.

It was dyed.

It was pressed.

It was measured.

It was designed.

It was cut.

It was sewed.

It was made by

Shorty the shearer

Spike the spinner

William the weaver

Clarence the colorist

Dick the dyer

Pete the presser

Doris the designer

Pat the pattern-maker

Carl the cutter

Olga the operator

Fanny the finisher

and many others.

It belonged to

   Mr. Tick who sold it to

   Mr. Tack who sold it to

   Mr. Toe who sold it to

   Mr. Bing who sold it to

   Mr. Bang who sold it to

you.

And now you wear it.

Your coat was not made by one worker alone. It was not made by one machine alone. It was not made in one place alone. It was made by many workers at different machines in different places—all working together.

This is the story of your coat.

Do you still think it is just an ordinary coat?